Building Essential Writing Skills

GRADE 4

New York • Toronto • London • Auckland • Sydney
Mexico City • New Delhi • Hong Kong • Buenos Aires

Writers: Jenny Wilsen, Lisa Benjamin
Editors: Maria L. Chang, Jenny Wilsen
Cover design: Tannaz Fassihi; Cover art: Eefje Kuijl
Interior design: Shekhar Kapur; Interior art: QBS Learning
Produced with QBS Learning

ISBN: 978-0-545-85042-1
Copyright © 2017 by Scholastic Inc.
All rights reserved.
Printed in the U.S.A.
First printing, January 2017.

1 2 3 4 5 6 7 8 9 10   40   25 24 23 22 21 20 19 18 17

Table of Contents

Table of Contents

Introduction

Help students master key writing skills with these standards-based activities designed to help them become successful writers. The fun, engaging reproducible pages are grouped into packets that provide targeted practice in writing sentences, organizing paragraphs, planning to write, drafting different types of texts, reviewing and improving writing, and revising and editing. Use the lesson to introduce the skills in each packet, then have students complete the pages to reinforce the lesson. As they work through the packets, students learn and practice important skills and concepts, such as types of sentences, punctuation, grammar, word choice, distinguishing fact from opinion, sequencing, adding details, and much more.

These versatile, ready-to-use practice pages can be used in many other ways:

- Select an activity page for use as a "do now" activity to help get students settled first thing in the morning. Simply stack copies of the page on a table for students to pick up as they enter the room. Then allow a specific amount of time, such as five minutes, for them to complete the activity.

- Preview the day's lesson with a related skills page. You can use the activity to find out what students already know about the topic.

- Alternatively, you can use an activity page to review a previously learned lesson, assess what students have learned, and determine where they need further instruction.

- Assign a skills page for students to complete independently, with a partner, in small groups, or for homework.

An answer key is provided at the back of the book so you can review answers with students. In doing so, you provide opportunities to discuss, reinforce, or extend skills to other lessons. Students can also share their responses and strategies in small groups. This collaboration will enable them to deepen their understanding or clarify any misunderstandings they may have about the skill or the writing process.

Meeting the Standards

The activities in this book meet the following standards for Grade 4.

Writing

Students will:

- Write opinion pieces on topics or texts, supporting a point of view with reasons and information.
- Introduce a topic or text clearly, state an opinion, and create an organizational structure in which related ideas are grouped to support the writer's purpose.
- Provide reasons that are supported by facts and details.
- Link opinion and reasons using words and phrases (e.g., *for instance, in order to*).
- Provide a concluding statement or section related to the opinion presented.
- Write informative/explanatory texts to examine a topic and convey ideas and information clearly.
- Introduce a topic clearly and group related information in paragraphs and sections.
- Develop the topic with facts, definitions, concrete details, quotations, or other information and examples related to the topic.
- Link ideas within categories of information using words and phrases (e.g., *for example, also*).
- Use precise language and domain-specific vocabulary to inform about or explain the topic.
- Provide a concluding statement or section related to the information or explanation presented.
- Write narratives to develop real or imagined experiences or events using effective technique, descriptive details, and clear event sequences.
- Establish a situation and introduce a narrator and/or characters; organize an event sequence that unfolds naturally.
- Use dialogue and description to develop experiences and events or show the response of characters to situations.
- Use a variety of transitional words and phrases to manage the sequence of events.
- Use concrete words and phrases and sensory details to convey experiences and events precisely.
- Provide a conclusion that follows from the narrated experiences or events.
- Produce clear and coherent writing in which the development and organization are appropriate to the task, purpose, and audience.
- With guidance and support from peers and adults, develop and strengthen writing as needed by planning, revising, editing, or rewriting.
- Recall information from experiences or gather information from print and digital sources; take brief notes on sources and sort evidence into provided categories.

Language

Students will:

- Form and use the progressive verb tenses.
- Use modal auxiliaries to convey various conditions.
- Form and use prepositional phrases.
- Produce complete sentences, recognizing and correcting inappropriate fragments and run-ons.
- Correctly use frequently confused words (e.g., *to, too, two; there, their*).
- Use correct capitalization.
- Use commas and quotation marks to mark direct speech and quotations from a text.
- Use a comma before a coordinating conjunction in a compound sentence.
- Spell grade-appropriate words correctly, consulting references as needed.
- Choose punctuation for effect.
- Demonstrate understanding of figurative language, word relationships, and nuances in word meanings.
- Recognize and explain the meaning of common idioms, adages, and proverbs.
- Use accurately grade-appropriate general academic and domain-specific words and phrases, including those that signal precise actions, emotions, or states of being and that are basic to a particular topic.

Lesson 1: Strong Sentences

Objective
Students will review basic sentence structure and types of sentences. They will practice writing sentences.

Standards
Produce complete sentences, recognizing and correcting inappropriate fragments and run-ons.

What You Need
Copies of this packet for each student; whiteboard and markers

What to Do
1. Write the following sentences on the board:

> *The Great Pyramids are in Egypt.*
> *Have you ever seen a picture of the pyramids?*
> *Read this article about the pyramids to learn more about them.*
> *The Egyptian pyramids are one of the wonders of the world!*

2. Tell students there are four main types of sentences, and they each serve a different purpose. Point to the first sentence and call on a volunteer to read it aloud. Explain that it is a **declarative sentence**—it states a fact or detail. Invite another volunteer to read aloud the second sentence. Explain that it is an **interrogative sentence**—it asks a question and ends in a question mark. Point to the third sentence and have a volunteer read it aloud. Explain that it is an **imperative sentence**—it gives a command, telling someone to do something. Have another volunteer read aloud the last sentence. Explain that it is an **exclamatory sentence**—it makes an excited remark and often ends with an exclamation point. Distribute copies of "Gone to the Dogs!" (page 8) to give students practice in identifying the different types of sentences.

3. Explain to students that every sentence must include a subject and a predicate. The **subject** is who or what the sentence is about. The **predicate** tells what happens. In the first sentence on the board, circle "The Great Pyramids" and explain that this is the subject—it tells what the sentence is about. Underline "are in Egypt." Explain that this is the predicate—it includes a verb and all the words that relate to it. Explain that a sentence must include both a subject and a predicate to be complete. A sentence that is missing either one is called a **sentence fragment**. Have students identify and fix sentence fragments using "The Presidents of Mount Rushmore" (page 9).

4. Tell students that they will continue to work with different types of sentences. The other activity pages in this packet will help them learn how to expand sentences by adding details, identify and fix run-on sentences, use active and passive voice, and punctuate dialogue.

Name: _____ Date: _____

Gone to the Dogs!

Read this article. Circle the declarative sentences. Underline the interrogative sentences. Draw a box around the imperative sentences. Place a check mark in front of the exclamatory sentences.

This weekend, the Westwood Kennel hosted a dog show for our community. It was a fun evening! Have you ever been to a dog show? You should go to one sometime. It is a chance for dog owners to show off their animals and win prizes. Dogs of the same breed, or type, compete against one another. They are judged on their appearance. The terrier group was the most fun to watch! This dog show was held for a special purpose. Can you guess what it was? It raised money for our local animal shelter. If you didn't attend the show, it's not too late to give. Please donate to the shelter.

The Presidents of Mount Rushmore

Read a paragraph Kelly wrote about Mount Rushmore. Underline fragments, or incomplete sentences. On the lines below, rewrite the fragments as complete sentences.

A famous mountain in the United States is Mount Rushmore. It is famous because one side has the faces of four presidents carved into it. In the Black Hills region, which is located in South Dakota. If you want to know what George Washington, Thomas Jefferson, Abraham Lincoln, and Theodore Roosevelt look like, all you need to do is visit Mount Rushmore. About 400 workers and almost 15 years. This mountain is one of the most popular tourist destinations in America. The sculptor had big plans for the monument. Wanted to show the presidents from the waist up, but there wasn't enough money. Two million visitors every year! I've never been, but I hope to visit one day!

1. _____

2. _____

3. _____

4. _____

> Make sentences interesting by adding extra details, using adjectives, adverbs, and clauses. A **clause** is a phrase that has a verb. A relative pronoun, such as *who*, *what*, and *that*, can introduce a clause. For example: *The sunflower that I planted last month is now six feet tall!*

How Interesting!

Read the instructions below. Write your answers.

1. Circle the clauses in the sentence.

A seed, which is very small, can grow into a tree that is very tall.

_____

2. Combine the sentences below using a clause.

My brother planted a sunflower. It grew very tall.

_____

3. Add details to these sentences to make them more interesting. Write your sentences on the line.

Vegetables are nutritious.

_____

Farms grow the food people eat.

_____

Use proper punctuation and conjunctions to connect ideas in a sentence. To connect the ideas, you can use a semicolon (;) or a comma (,) with a **coordinating conjunction**, such as *and, or, so, but, since,* and *as.*

On the Road Again

Read the sentences. Connect the sentences using punctuation and/or coordinating conjunctions. The first one has been done for you.

1. Going on a road trip is exciting. It takes a lot of planning.

Going on a road trip is exciting, but it takes a lot of planning.

2. It's always a good idea to map out your trip. There are apps that can help you.

_____

3. You might want to go to an amusement park. You could go to the beach.

_____

4. Last year, Mom wanted to go to a national park. We went to Yellowstone.

_____

5. We got lost. Dad got off the wrong exit.

_____

6. Luckily we found a gas station. The people there told us how to get back on the right road.

_____

Name: _____   Date: _____

A **run-on sentence** contains too many ideas joined together without using proper punctuation. You can fix a run-on sentence by breaking it into two or more sentences or by using a comma and a conjunction, such as *and, but, or,* or *so,* to separate ideas.

A Rainy Saturday Afternoon

Read each sentence. Check the box if it is a run-on sentence. Then rewrite it as two complete sentences or use a comma and conjunction to separate the ideas.

☐ **1.** We planned to have a picnic on Saturday it started to rain.

_____

☐ **2.** So we changed our plans, and we decided to go to the movies.

_____

☐ **3.** We drove to the theater there was a lot of traffic.

_____

☐ **4.** The movie had already started by the time we arrived.

_____

☐ **5.** We gave up on that plan too we went for pizza instead.

_____

Building Essential Writing Skills: Grade 4 © Scholastic Inc.

Name: _____ Date: _____

 Sentences can have either an **active** or a **passive voice**. In an active sentence, the subject does an action. For example: *I broke the computer.*
In a passive sentence, the action usually happens to the subject. For example: *The computer was broken by me.*

So Many Spices

Read this paragraph about Indian food. Find the four passive sentences and rewrite them as active sentences.

Indian food is delicious, probably because it contains so many different kinds of spices and sauces. Spices come from different parts of plants, such as leaves, flowers, fruits, seeds, and bark. Even roots are dug out of the ground to spice our meals. Spices can be used in recipes whole and raw, like cloves of garlic, or they can be dried and made into a powder, such as turmeric powder. Spices are used by cooks in their recipes to add special flavors. For example, cumin makes foods nutty, and mint makes foods cool. Indian sauces are made using all kinds of spices. Cooks blend the spices with butter (called *ghee*), cream, coconut milk, vegetables, and more.

1. _____

   _____

2. _____

   _____

3. _____

   _____

4. _____

   _____

Building Essential Writing Skills: Grade 4 © Scholastic Inc.

Quotation marks are used to show what a person said exactly. Use a comma to separate a quote from who says it. The comma—as well as end punctuation, such as a period, question mark, or exclamation point—goes inside the quotation mark.

You Can Quote Me on That!

Look at the sentences. Check the box if the sentence uses the correct punctuation. If the sentence is not correct, write the sentence correctly on the line.

☐ **1.** "Put the cat down"! Kevin screamed. "He bites"!

_____

☐ **2.** "I wish," the poor girl started to say, "I had a beautiful dress to wear to the party."

_____

☐ **3.** Yesterday, my friend Gillian asked me. "Do you know what a monarch butterfly looks like!"

_____

☐ **4.** "The sun is way too bright Lillian complained. I need my sunglasses."

_____

☐ **5.** Turn up the music" Jason said to his brother.

_____

☐ **6.** Is anyone there? Henry asked, "not sure if he was alone in the dark room."
   I sure hope this room isn't haunted.

_____

Building Essential Writing Skills: Grade 4 © Scholastic Inc.

Lesson 2: Powerful Paragraphs

Objective
Students will review basic paragraph structure and types of sentences. They will practice writing paragraphs.

Standards
Produce clear and coherent writing in which the development and organization are appropriate to task, purpose, and audience.

What You Need
Copies of this packet for each student; whiteboard and markers

What to Do

1. Tell students that a **paragraph** is a group of sentences that focuses on a single theme, or main idea. A paragraph usually begins with a **topic sentence** that presents the main idea. It includes **supporting sentences** that provide additional information about this main idea. The **concluding sentence** wraps up the paragraph.

2. Call on a volunteer to read the following paragraph aloud:

   Where can you find the biggest wall in the world? In China! Two thousand years ago, China's emperor decided to build a strong wall to keep enemies away. He had people mend old walls and erect new ones out of stone and mud. Then they connected all the walls into one great wall that was 3,000 miles long! Over the next thousand years, other emperors extended the wall until it stretched for more than 13,000 miles. Much of the Great Wall of China still stands today.

3. Identify the first sentence as the topic sentence. It introduces the main idea of the paragraph. Ask students what they think is the paragraph's main idea. *(The Great Wall of China)* Distribute copies of "That Sounds Interesting" (page 16) to give students practice in writing introductory sentences.

4. Discuss how the other sentences in the paragraph support the main idea with additional facts and details. Explain that supporting sentences should relate to the topic and not introduce any new ideas. Hand out copies of "Stick to the Main Idea" (page 17) to reinforce this concept.

5. Point out the use of transitional words and phrases, such as "Then" and "Over the next thousand years" to connect ideas. Use "Protecting Panda Bears" (page 19) and "What Came First?" (page 20) to give students practice in using transitional words and phrases.

6. Finally, point out how the concluding sentence wraps up the paragraph. Distribute "Where's the Ending" (page 21) and "A Day Out in the Water" (page 22) for practice in writing conclusions.

> ★ Use the first sentence in your paragraph to get your reader interested in the topic. You can ask a question, state your opinion, use a quote, or explain how you first learned about the topic.

That Sounds Interesting

Write an introduction sentence for the topics below.

1. The First Day of School

_____

_____

2. Endangered Animals

_____

_____

3. Wild Weather

_____

_____

4. Volunteering at an Animal Shelter

_____

_____

5. Living in Space

_____

_____

Powerful paragraphs focus on one **main idea**. They do not include extra information. For instance, a paragraph about ice cream should not suddenly switch to discussing baseball.

Stick to the Main Idea

Read the beginning of the following paragraph. Then choose three sentences from below that could be included. Write them to complete the paragraph.

A volcano may look like an ordinary mountain. But if the volcano is active, smoke, ash, and hot lava can erupt from it. An eruption can be very dangerous.

_____

_____

_____

_____

_____

_____

a. The ash gets into the air, making it difficult to breathe.

b. An earthquake is another kind of natural disaster.

c. During an earthquake, the ground can shake violently.

d. People cannot easily escape an area when a volcano is erupting.

e. Hot lava can burn everything in its path, causing a lot of damage.

f. If an earthquake happens in the ocean, it can create a huge wave of water.

Name: _____   Date: _____

 Powerful paragraphs must include **supporting details**. They add information to your topic sentence. They also make your writing stronger and more interesting.

Add Some Information

Read each topic sentence below. Then write two sentences with supporting details that could be included in a paragraph about it.

1. There are a lot of fun activities to do during the summer.

    a. _____

    b. _____

2. Dogs make great pets for several reasons.

    a. _____

    b. _____

3. People do different things to celebrate Thanksgiving.

    a. _____

    b. _____

4. The big snowstorm brought the entire city to a stop.

    a. _____

    b. _____

Building Essential Writing Skills: Grade 4 © Scholastic Inc.

> **Transitional words and phrases** help connect your ideas. Without transitions, the reader might not understand how sentences relate to each other.

Protecting Panda Bears

Read the passage. Fill in the blanks with transitional words or phrases from the box below.

What Transitional Words or Phrases Do			
Give more details	**Show contrast**		**Show effect**
In addition	But	Even though	As a result
In fact	However	Despite this	
For one thing	On the contrary		

Giant panda bears were once *endangered*, or in danger of dying out. Why?

_____, people destroyed much of their *habitat*, or the place where

they live. Giant pandas live in bamboo forests in China. _____,

people cut down forests to make room for farms and housing. _____,

hunters in the past killed pandas. _____ the government made it

illegal to kill pandas, some bears still get caught in traps meant for other animals.

_____ there's still hope for giant pandas. The government created protected

reserves, where pandas can live safely. _____, pandas are slowly

making a comeback. _____, in September 2016 giant pandas

were taken off the endangered species list. That doesn't mean they're out of trouble.

_____, giant pandas are still at risk. _____,

if we continue to work together, we can save pandas and other animals from dying out.

A story is a **sequence of events**, or a list of actions that happen in a certain order. Writers use transitional words or phrases to tell readers what happened first, second, and third. Transitional words also tell when actions happen at the same time.

What Came First?

Write a paragraph about the first day of school. Write the sentences in order in the boxes. Start each sentence using a transitional word or phrase from the list below.

first	next	then	last	finally
in the end	before	after/afterwards	later (on)	since
meanwhile	until (after/before)	all of a sudden	suddenly	immediately
			at this/that instant	

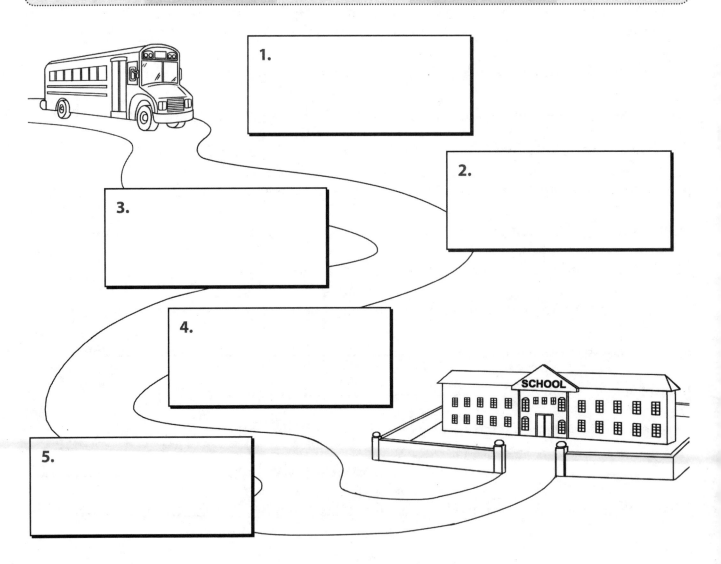

A **concluding sentence** is the last sentence in your paragraph and tells the reader your final thoughts on your topic. It should only contain ideas that were already mentioned in the paragraph. Don't add any new ideas in your conclusion.

Where's the Ending?

Read the paragraph below. Underline the concluding sentence.

People should reuse containers instead of throwing them away. Many containers can be cleaned and used again. For example, we can use a glass jar that held spaghetti sauce to store things, such as loose nails or screws. We can also turn an empty milk jug into a bird feeder. There are many ways we can reuse containers.

Now read each paragraph below. Write a concluding sentence for each one.

I think we should grow flower gardens to attract honeybees. I read that honeybees are disappearing. This makes me very sad. If everyone grew the flowers that honeybees love, like echinacea, sunflowers, and black-eyed Susans, the bees might come back.

_____

_____

Saving water is not that difficult when you put your mind to it. You can take fast showers. When brushing your teeth, you can turn off the water. You can also use rainwater to water your plants.

_____

_____

Name: _____ Date: _____

 In your conclusion, you want to remind your reader about your main topic. You can also tell readers why the topic is important and then give your own opinion about the topic.

A Day Out on the Water

Jake is writing an article about how to fish. He wrote about fishing rods, worms and other kinds of bait, and how to clean fish. But he doesn't know how to end his article. Help Jake write different endings. Then circle which ending you think he should use.

1. Write a concluding sentence telling readers what they should do next.

_____

2. Write a concluding sentence telling readers why learning how to fish is important.

_____

3. Write a concluding sentence telling readers why YOU think this topic is important.

_____

4. Write a concluding sentence summarizing the article in that one sentence.

_____

Lesson 3: Getting Ready to Write

Objective
Students will choose a topic, brainstorm, and gather and organize information for different types of writing.

Standards
With guidance and support from peers and adults, develop and strengthen writing as needed by planning, revising, and editing.

What You Need
Copies of this packet for each student; whiteboard and markers

What to Do

1. Explain to students that writers do a lot of preparation work before they start writing. **Prewriting** includes picking a topic, gathering information, and organizing ideas.

2. Tell students that when deciding what to write about, they should choose a topic they're interested in. Their topic should have a focus. If students are writing an opinion piece, they should pick a topic in which they have a strong point of view. Distribute copies of "What Should We Do?" (page 24). Read aloud the first problem. Invite students to discuss what they think Denise should do about her topic. Then have students work in pairs or small groups to complete the rest of the page, encouraging them to discuss their thoughts.

3. Distribute copies of "In My Opinion . . ." (page 25). Explain that this page can be used to jot down reasons for an opinion before writing an opinion text. If necessary, review how to use the organizer.

4. Using "The Coral Reefs Are Dying" (page 26), encourage students to do some research to complete the organizer. They can also use "I'm the Expert!" (page 27) to find and organize information for an informative text. Explain that they should always use reliable sources to find information they need and to keep track of their sources.

5. Distribute the other organizers in this packet to help students brainstorm and organize their ideas for opinion, informative, and narrative texts. Then set aside students' organizers, explaining that they might want to use some of them later when writing a draft.

⭐ Choose a topic that you know or care about. If you do not know much about your topic, do research.

What Should We Do?

Denise, Casey, and Vincent are having problems writing about the topic they chose. Write what you think each of them should do.

1. Denise chose the topic "People should protect dolphins from being caught in tuna nets." Denise does not really care about dolphins. She chose this topic because her teacher likes dolphins. What should she do?

_____

_____

_____

2. Casey chose to write about a factory in his town that causes pollution. He went to the library, but could not find any information. He asked his neighbors, and no one had any facts. The people at the factory did not want to talk to him. His essay is due next week. What should he do?

_____

_____

_____

3. Vincent chose to write about gardening. He and his mother grow vegetables in their home garden, and he enjoys eating all the food he grows. He has a lot to say about gardening. What should he do?

_____

_____

_____

Name: _____   Date: _____

In My Opinion . . .

Choose a topic that you have an opinion about. Write the reasons for your opinion in the thought bubbles.

Opinion_____

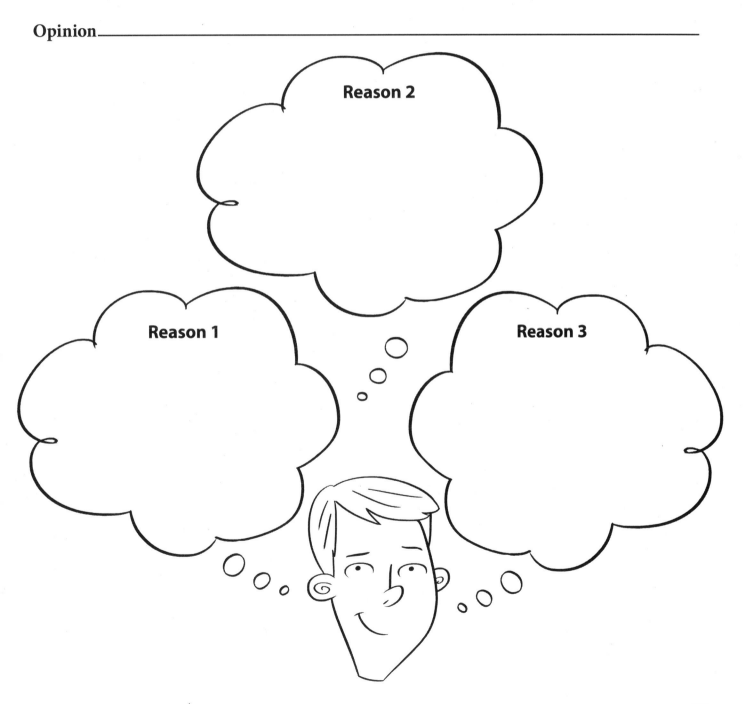

Reason 2

Reason 1

Reason 3

Name: _____   Date: _____

 To organize a problem-solution paragraph, you first need to think of a problem. Then think about ways to fix the problem.

The Coral Reefs Are Dying

Charlie is writing a paragraph about how coral reefs are dying in the oceans. He has started to fill in a graphic organizer to organize his paragraph. Do some research to help Charlie write three possible solutions.

Problem	The coral reefs are turning white and dying. Oceans are becoming too hot and acidic for the ocean plants and animals. Pollution and overfishing are also part of the problem.
Solution #1	
Solution #2	
Solution #3	

Name: _____ Date: _____

I'm the Expert!

Think of a topic you would like to know more about. Become the expert by getting answers to fully understand your topic. Fill in the graphic organizer with the information you learned.

Topic: _____

Who?

What?

Where?

When?

Why?

Plan It Out

Choose a topic for an informative text. Make sure you have enough details to support your topic. Use the graphic organizer to plan your paragraph.

My Topic

_____

Introduction _____

Point 1 _____

Detail 1 _____

_____

Detail 2 _____

_____

Point 2 _____

Detail 1 _____

_____

Detail 2 _____

_____

Point 3 _____

Detail 1 _____

_____

Detail 2 _____

_____

Conclusion _____

Name: _____   Date: _____

 Sometimes an idea about an event becomes the basis of a **narrative text**, or story. Use an organizer to write down ideas about your story.

Fill the Sky

Imagine you are writing a story about going up in a hot-air balloon.
Use the graphic organizer to plan your story.

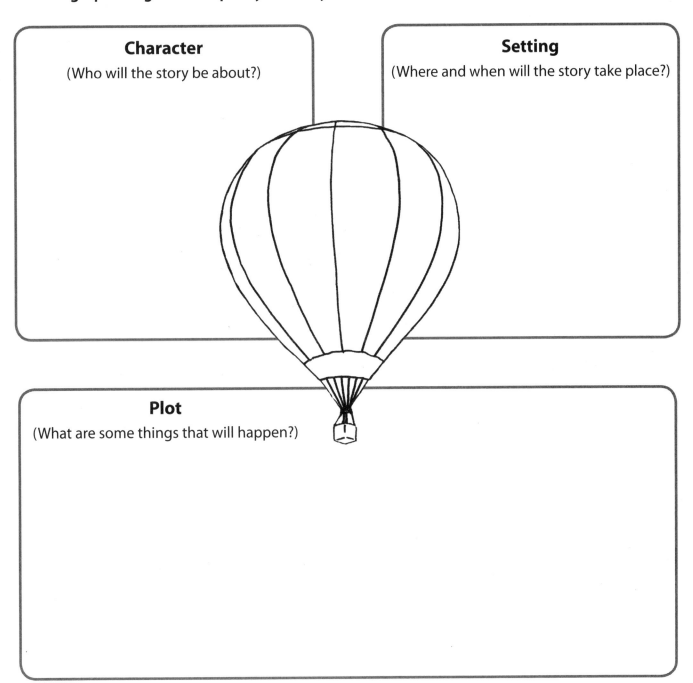

Character
(Who will the story be about?)

Setting
(Where and when will the story take place?)

Plot
(What are some things that will happen?)

Lesson 4: Purpose for Writing

Objective

Students will identify different kinds of writing and set a purpose for writing.

Standards

- Write opinion pieces on topics or texts, supporting a point of view with reasons and information.
- Write informative/explanatory texts to examine a topic and convey ideas and information clearly.
- Write narratives to develop real or imagined experiences or events using effective technique, descriptive details, and clear event sequences.

What You Need

Copies of this packet for each student; whiteboard and markers

What to Do

1. Tell students that writers always have a **purpose**, or reason, for writing. They try to choose the best way to present their topics in order to reflect their purpose. For example, a text about life in the future might work best as a short story that entertains readers. A text about recycling could be an informative piece that gives facts or an opinion piece that tells a point of view. It is important for writers to consider what they want readers to know or experience when they set a purpose for writing. Distribute copies of "Going on an Adventure" (page 31) to give students practice in deciding what type of writing works best for different topics.

2. Explain to students that the purpose for writing an **opinion text** is to share what they think or feel about a particular topic. They should provide reasons for the opinion and support those reasons with facts and details. Use "Goats Make Great Pets," "Support Your Point of View," and "Our Carbon Footprint" (pages 32–34) to help reinforce this concept. Then distribute copies of "What's Your Opinion?" (page 35) for students to draft an opinion text.

3. Tell students that in an **informative text**, the writer shares facts and information that have been gathered through reading and research. As much as possible, writers should not include their opinion in an informative text. Have students complete "Ocean Trash" (page 36), then distribute copies of "Write About It!" (page 37) for students to write an informative text.

4. Tell students that a **narrative text** tells a story with characters, a setting, and a plot. The story can be real or made up. Events in the story should follow a logical order. Distribute copies of "Let's Get This Story Started," "An Alien Encounter," and "Davey Learns to Swim" (pages 38–40) to review story elements. Use the other activity pages in this packet to help students learn about points of view, using dialogue to liven up writing, and more. They can use the writing template (page 44) for their drafts.

Name: _____ Date: _____

 There are different reasons for writing. In **opinion writing**, you state what you think or feel about a topic and give reasons why. In **informative writing**, you share facts and information about a topic. In **narrative writing**, you tell a story.

Going on an Adventure

Read each topic below. Decide what type of writing it is—opinion, informative, or narrative.

1. One family's hiking adventure

_____

2. The history of an old castle

_____

3. Why everyone should try mountain climbing

_____

4. A boy discovers a treasure in his backyard

_____

5. The routes taken by an early explorer

_____

Name: _____   Date: _____

Goats Make Great Pets

Read the paragraph that Jeff wrote to convince his parents to let him have a goat as a pet. Answer the questions below.

(1) I think a goat would make a good pet because it is more eco-friendly than a dog or a cat. (2) First, goats eat grass all day and all night. (3) We could sell the lawnmower. (4) Since goats will eat anything, we will need to tie him up to keep him from eating Mom's roses. (5) Second, goat poop would help our plants grow. (6) However, we might have to watch where we're stepping when we're out in the yard. (7) Third, a goat could be trained to do work, like pulling a wagon. (8) These are just some of the reasons why I think a goat would make a great pet.

1. Which sentence states Jeff's opinion?   Sentence # _____

2. What are Jeff's three arguments?

Argument 1: _____

_____

Argument 2: _____

_____

Argument 3: _____

_____

3. Which sentence could be added as a supporting detail?
   a. We could load the wagon with groceries or even gardening tools.
   b. Another reason is we can use goat milk to make cheese.
   c. This is why I think goats are better than lawnmowers.

Name: _____   Date: _____

Support Your Point of View

Read the two opinions below. Then decide which opinion each fact supports by writing A or B on the blank.

Opinion A	Opinion B
Everyone should recycle paper, metal, and plastic to help protect the environment.	Circuses should not include wild animals in their acts.

1. Animals are often used to perform dangerous tricks. _____

2. Lions and tigers have been known to attack their trainers. _____

3. Creating landfills to collect garbage takes up a lot of space. _____

4. Items made from plastic take a very long time to break down. _____

5. Reusing paper goods instead of throwing them away helps save trees. _____

6. Animals that live in the wild are healthier than animals that live in cages. _____

7. Elephants have run away from circuses, putting communities at risk. _____

8. Plastic bags that fall into the ocean can kill fish and other sea creatures. _____

Name: _____   Date: _____

 Whether you introduce two or three points in your paragraph, make sure each point is important and related to your main topic.

Our Carbon Footprint

Kevin wrote all the main points of his essay, but he got frustrated because he had too many supporting details. Help him by writing the missing information from the list below in the graphic organizer. Cross out the two details he doesn't need.

Introduction: My family cares about the environment, so we work hard to keep our *carbon footprint** small.

First, we buy our fruits and vegetables from local farms.

_____

_____

Second, we ride bikes to nearby places.

_____

_____

Third, we turn on the air conditioner only when we are in the house.

_____

_____

Conclusion: My family tries hard not to be wasteful.

*A carbon footprint is the amount of energy a person uses to live and travel.

1. You waste energy when you keep the air conditioner on when you are not home.
2. Our food doesn't have to travel from faraway places.
3. My friends ride their bikes to school, to the park, and around the neighborhood.
4. Driving a car uses a lot of energy and releases tons of carbon dioxide into the atmosphere every year.
5. Dad says the air in our city is very clean, so we don't have to worry about pollution.

What's Your Opinion?

Write a first draft of your opinion paragraph.

_____

_____

_____

_____

_____

_____

_____

_____

_____

_____

_____

Now check your work.

☐ Do you have an introductory sentence?

☐ Do you state your opinion clearly?

☐ Does your paragraph discuss only one main idea?

☐ Do you use facts to support your opinion and explain your ideas?

☐ Do you have a concluding sentence?

☐ Do all of your sentences include a subject and a verb?

☐ Have you checked your spelling?

☐ Have you checked your punctuation?

Name: _____   Date: _____

 When writing an **informative text**, include facts and details that support the main idea. As much as possible, do not include your opinion.

Ocean Trash

Read this article about plastic in the ocean. Then answer the questions below.

Every year, hundreds of thousands of turtles, seabirds, and other marine animals get sick when they eat or get tangled in ocean trash. Many of them die. That's a terrible tragedy! One of the biggest problems is plastic. A recent study estimated that more than 500 million pounds of plastic trash are floating around the world's oceans. How does it get there? A lot of it starts out as litter on land. Then wind and rain sweep it into the ocean. Once plastic is in the water, it can stay there for decades. Marine animals often mistake pieces of plastic for food. Sometimes they choke on them. The trash can also block their digestive tract, so the animals can starve. Animals can also become tangled in large pieces of trash.

1. What is the main idea of this article?
   a. There's too much plastic trash in the ocean.
   b. Plastic trash in the ocean is harming marine animals.
   c. Marine animals are dying.
   d. People should use less plastic.

2. Which detail supports the main idea?
   a. More than 500 million pounds of plastic trash are floating around the world's oceans.
   b. Plastic starts out as litter on land.
   c. Marine animals often mistake pieces of plastic for food and can choke on them.
   d. Plastic can stay in the water for decades.

3. Cross out the sentence that is an opinion and should be taken out.

4. What other information could be added to this article? Write your ideas here.

_____

_____

Building Essential Writing Skills: Grade 4 © Scholastic Inc.

Write About It!

Write a first draft of your informative text.

_____

_____

_____

_____

_____

_____

_____

_____

_____

_____

_____

Now check your work.

☐ Do you use facts and specific details?

☐ Do you connect your ideas?

☐ Do all of your sentences include a subject and a verb?

☐ Do your verbs have the correct tenses?

☐ Have you checked your spelling?

☐ Have you checked your punctuation?

Name: _____   Date: _____

> **Narrative** is the literary term for a story. A good story contains five key elements: character (who the story is about), setting (where and when the story takes place), plot (what the story is about), conflict (the main problem), and theme (the moral or lesson of the story).

Let's Get This Story Started

Philip is writing a story about a group of friends who build a tree house. Using the terms in the box, write the story element that Philip's ideas refer to.

Setting	Plot	Character	Conflict	Theme

1. Philip wants his story to take place in a backyard. Which story element does this refer to?

_____

2. In Philip's story, the boys get stuck in the tree because the ladder they built wasn't strong

enough. Which story element does this refer to? _____

3. Philip wants to talk about friendship and trust in his story. Which story element does this

refer to? _____

4. Philip's story is about a group of friends who build a tree house one summer.

Which story element does this refer to? _____

5. One of the boys in Philip's story is named Fred. He likes to stay up late at night.

Which story element does this refer to? _____

Name: _____   Date: _____

Readers want to know where and when your story takes place (setting) and who the story is about (characters). Give readers this information in the beginning of your story.

An Alien Encounter

Imagine a story about two sisters who meet a space alien. Answer the questions below. Then write the story on another sheet of paper.

1. Will the story take place in the past, the present, or the future?

_____

2. Does the story take place in a real or imaginary place?

_____

3. How much time passes between the beginning and the end of the story?

_____

4. Describe one of the characters.

_____

_____

5. Should readers like or dislike the characters?

_____

6. How do the sisters feel about the alien?

_____

_____

Name: _____ Date: _____

Each part of the plot is important to get and keep readers' attention.

Davey Learns to Swim

Read about the different parts of a plot.

Exposition	The part of the story that introduces the setting and main characters
Point of Conflict	The part in the story where the main problem begins
Rising Action	A series of actions that are caused because of the problem
Climax	The part where the main characters have to solve the problem
Falling Action	A series of actions done by the main characters to solve the problem
Resolution	The part when the problem is solved and the characters can continue their lives

Look at Davey's story below. Match each key story element to the correct description.

1. Exposition

2. Point of Conflict

3. Climax

4. Resolution

a. Davey cannot swim. His friends make fun of him.

b. Davey is comfortable swimming in the ocean with friends.

c. Davey is at a pool party with some friends.

d. Davey starts taking a swim class and becomes a good swimmer.

> A story is usually told from one of two different points of view. In **first person**, the main character tells the story using pronouns like *I* and *we*. In **third person**, someone else tells the story using pronouns like *he*, *she*, and *they*.

Who's Telling the Story?

Answer the questions below.

1. Read the story below. From which point of view is it written? How do you know?

_____

    My brother likes to play video games. One day, the television sucked him up, and he became one of the characters in the game. I used the controller to make him jump and move in the game. It was a lot of fun—for me!

2. Rewrite this story in the first person.

    She looked around her bedroom for her cell phone, but couldn't find it. If only she remembered she had left it at her best friend's house.

_____

_____

_____

3. Rewrite this story in the third person.

    Oh, no! I didn't jump high enough and didn't catch the ball. As I fell to the ground, the other team cheered, and my teammates put their heads down in shame.

_____

_____

_____

Name: _____   Date: _____

You can explain what your characters are doing either through dialogue or through a description—or both. For example: *Karin said she wanted to go to the movies. Karin said, "I want to go to the movies."*

Fetch the Stick!

Jenny wrote a story about a barking dog, but her story doesn't have any dialogue. Rewrite her story with some dialogue. Remember to use quotation marks.

One Saturday morning, Mom took Timmy and their dog Rufus to the park. When they got to the park, Rufus wouldn't stop barking. Timmy asked Mom why Rufus was barking. Mom didn't know. She suggested they give Rufus water and a treat, but he just kept barking. Timmy said he didn't think that worked. They had no idea what the dog wanted!

Rufus yipped one more time, and Mom finally understood! She told Timmy that Rufus wanted to play fetch. She laughed as she threw a stick. They played for a while, and then decided to go home for lunch. Timmy said he had a lot of fun!

_____

_____

_____

_____

_____

_____

_____

Name: _____   Date: _____

Here's What Happened . . .

Write a first draft of your narrative text.

_____

_____

_____

_____

_____

_____

_____

_____

_____

_____

Now check your work.

☐ Do you start the story with an exposition about the setting and characters?

☐ Do your characters speak? Is your dialogue formatted correctly?

☐ Do you use descriptive language?

☐ Did you check your spelling?

☐ Do your sentences start with a capital letter and have end punctuation?

Name: _____   Date: _____

Title: _____

_____

_____

_____

_____

_____

_____

_____

_____

_____

_____

_____

_____

_____

_____

_____

_____

_____

Lesson 5: Pump Up Your Writing

Objective
Students will review parts of speech and use them to pump up their writing.

Standard
Demonstrate command of the conventions of standard English grammar and usage when writing.

What You Need
Copies of this packet for each student; whiteboard and markers

What to Do

1. Write the following on the board:

Noun   *Adjective*   *Adverb*
Verb   *Preposition*

2. Review the parts of speech with students. Explain that different words have different functions in sentences. Knowing how to use the various parts of speech properly can help pump up their writing. Point to the word "Noun" and ask students to define it. *(A noun is a person, place, or thing.)* Ask students to name some nouns and write a few examples on the board next to the term "Noun." Repeat this process with each part of speech: ask students to define the term, provide examples, and write them on the board.

3. Explain that an **adjective** is a word that describes a noun or pronoun. An **adverb** is a word that describes a verb, adjective, or another adverb. Writers use these describing words to add details and make their writing come alive. Distribute copies of "Visiting Grandma in Space," "How Would You Describe That?" and "Hong Kong Is Sensational" (pages 46–48) to give students practice in using adjectives and adverbs.

4. Tell students that a **verb** tells an action or a state of being. **Helping verbs** can add meaning to a verb or change its tense. Use "Don't Deforest the Earth!" (page 49) to help reinforce this concept. "My Painting Is Coming Alive" (page 50) gives students practice in identifying **progressive verbs**.

5. Explain that a **preposition** connects a noun or pronoun to another noun. A **prepositional phrase** combines a preposition with a noun to describe location, direction, time, or relationship. Writers also use prepositional phrases to add descriptive details to their writing. Distribute copies of "A Trip to Canada" (page 51) to help students understand how prepositional phrases are used.

6. Tell students that writers use many other "tricks" to pump up their writing, including using specific vocabulary and figurative language. Use the other activity pages in this packet to help reinforce this lesson.

Name: _____   Date: _____

 An **adjective** describes a noun, including feelings.
An **adverb** describes a verb or an adjective and often ends in *-ly*.

Visiting Grandma in Space

Read the story. Circle the correct adjective or adverb in the parentheses.

"Ticket, please!" I reached into the pocket of my *(heavy/heavily)* red coat
(1)
to find my ticket. The ticket had an
(enormous/enormously) moon printed on it.
(2)

"So you're going to the moon, are you?" the conductor asked. I nodded
(nervous/nervously). "Don't worry. I'll tell
(3)
you when it's your stop."

The conductor smiled before walking away. Right then, the rocket ship
(sudden/suddenly) jolted forward and then
(4)
backwards. The lights flashed, and bags started falling to the floor. If I was nervous before, I was *(frightened/frightening/*
(5)
frighteningly) now!

I was so *(glad/gladly)* I had kept my
(6)
bag under my seat. Inside my bag was my prized possession: my grandmother's locket. But when I looked in my bag, the

locket wasn't there! I had to find it. I started to unbuckle my seat belt when I heard the man across the aisle from me say, "Is this what you're looking for?"

I couldn't believe it! It was my
(lucky/luckily) day! The man had found my
(7)
locket! I *(immediate/immediately)* thanked
(8)
him and put the locket around my neck.

"Everyone, attention!" the conductor called out. "We just hit an air pocket. Please sit down and stay *(calm/calming/calmly)*."
(9)
That's *(exact/exactly)* what I did.
(10)

My grandmother was waiting for me on the platform. "Look, Grams. I'm wearing your locket," I said, *(proud/proudly)*
(11)
showing it to her.

"And you look *(beautiful/beautifully)*,
(12)
my dear," replied my grandmother.

Building Essential Writing Skills: Grade 4 © Scholastic Inc.

Name: _____ Date: _____

 Imagine a piece of fried chicken. Now, imagine a piece of juicy, crispy, golden-brown fried chicken. Which picture is more vivid and alive? The second description has more details, and readers can visualize the chicken more easily. Use details to make your writing more interesting.

How Would You Describe That?

Practice using description in your writing by answering the questions below.

1. How would you describe the beach?

_____

2. How would you describe your best friend?

_____

3. What does your classroom look like?

_____

4. Finish these sentences with as much description as you can.

When I'm really hungry, I like to eat _____

My dream house is _____

_____

5. Rewrite this sentence. Add description to make the sentence more interesting.

I loaned the girl my umbrella because she forgot to bring her raincoat.

_____

_____

Name: _____   Date: _____

Concrete words are specific words, like colors, shapes, and sizes. Everyone understands what you mean if you say "the six-foot-high walls were white." **Sensory details** use the five senses to describe something.

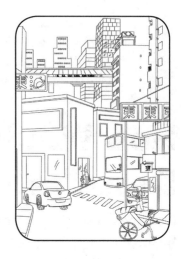

Hong Kong Is Sensational!

1. Read the sentences below. Write which sense (sight, smell, touch, hearing, taste) is used to describe the city.

• A mix of fragrances, from sweet to pungent, surround people as they walk through the open markets.

_____

• From far away, the city seems to glitter because of the many glass buildings reflecting the sunlight.

_____

• The waitress brought a plate of food that was slightly tangy, with a light, fruity flavor.

_____

• Honk! Screech! Ding-ding! There's never a second of silence in this busy city.

_____

• Cool, glossy, smooth tiles cover several walls in public spaces.

_____

2. Write a sentence describing a busy street. _____

_____

3. Write a sentence describing a piece of furniture. _____

_____

4. Write a sentence describing a caterpillar. _____

_____

Name: _____   Date: _____

 A **helping verb**, or auxiliary verb, adds extra meaning to the main verb. Helping verbs such as *be, have, do, can, could,* and *might* can change the tense of the verb. For example: I <u>am eating</u> a banana. I <u>have eaten</u> a banana.
Do can also add emphasis to the main verb. For example: <u>*Do take*</u> another cookie, Janet.

Don't Deforest the Earth!

Circle the auxiliary words. Underline the verbs. Draw an arrow from the auxiliary word to the verb it "helps."

1. If all the trees in the forest are destroyed, what would happen to all the animals that already live there?

2. About 30 percent of the land on Earth is covered with forests, and every minute, forests the size of 20 football fields are being cut down.

3. Researchers have developed many cancer-fighting medicines using plants in the rain forest, but almost half the world's rain forests are already gone.

4. Trees do produce a lot of the air we breathe, so we must stop deforestation as soon as possible.

Write a sentence using a helping verb.

_____

_____

_____

> Some stories are told using the **progressive tense**, as if the action is still in progress or happening now. Progressive tense verbs end with -ing. There is a present progressive tense and a past progressive tense.
>
> Present Progressive Tense: *Jason is riding his bike to Paul's house now.*
>
> Past Progressive Tense: *Jason was riding his bicycle to Paul's house when he fell and broke his leg.*

My Painting Is Coming Alive!

Keisha is writing a short story about an artist whose paintings come to life when she puts down her paintbrush. Underline the progressive verbs she uses in her story.

Leslie had been painting for hours, but she was still only halfway finished. She didn't know why she was painting such a dangerous scene. In her picture, the dinosaur was looking at fire pouring out of a volcano. The volcano was erupting! *If I put down my brush now, the dinosaur will jump off the paper and wreck my room*, Leslie thought. *And the volcano will be erupting in real life!* Leslie decided the only way she could stay alive would be to rip the paper in half. She was getting ready to tear the paper when her mother walked in.

"What a beautiful painting, darling! Why don't you come downstairs for a quick snack?"

"That sounds great!" Leslie replied. She started to put her brush down, and then stopped herself. "Uh . . . I'll be down in a minute, Mom. I am just finishing up."

Finish Keisha's story. Use progressive verbs in your sentences.

_____

_____

_____

Writers use **prepositional phrases** to add details to a sentence. A prepositional phrase is made by joining a preposition with a noun to tell the *where* or *when* of an object or activity. For example: <u>over</u> *the very tall fence* and <u>since</u> *the concert.*

A Trip to Canada

Marcus wrote an article about Canada. Circle the prepositions in his paragraph. Underline the prepositional phrases.

On the eastern coast of Canada is a tiny island called Prince Edward Island. My family visited the island last year, mostly because my older sister is obsessed with the Anne of Green Gables books. The author of the book grew up on the island, and her stories take place around the island, too. We rented a car from the airport and then took a ferry across the water to the island. You can drive from one side of the island to the other within a short time; however, we weren't bored. We found some beautiful, bright red cliffs along the edge of the island. They are red because the ground is clay. Below the cliffs was the ocean. Standing at the edge of the cliff, I felt like I was on top of the world.

Name: _____   Date: _____

 Linking words help connect your ideas. Without linking words, the reader might not understand how ideas connect to each other.

Making Connections

Choose the best linking word for each sentence. Draw lines to connect the correct linking word with the rest of the sentence.

1. The fishermen at the pier were selling all kinds of seafood,

(including)
(because)

clams and shrimp.

2. Larry would have gone swimming in the lake,

(due to)
(except that)

he forgot to bring his swimming trunks.

3. Spider webs are useful

(because)
(like)

they trap mosquitoes.

4. The pool is closed this afternoon

(due to)
(although)

a thunderstorm coming this way.

5. No one had enough energy left to go bike riding,

(and besides)
(including)

there wasn't enough time.

6. One reason we left early was that we were bored, and

(another)
(except)

was that we were hungry.

Name: _____   Date: _____

To sound authoritative, use the special words you learned while researching your topic.

Japan's Beautiful Volcano

Read Penelope's draft and help her revise her writing. Use her vocabulary notes to cross out phrases that can be replaced, and write the appropriate vocabulary word above them.

Mt. Fuji is the tallest mountain in Japan. It is located outside Tokyo, Japan's capital city, and has a height of 12,388 feet. The mountain, which is usually pictured with a top part covered with snow, is actually a volcano. The last time Mt. Fuji blew up was in 1707, a very long time ago.

A lot of people visit Mt. Fuji to hike. Visitors walk up to the very top of the mountain to see the sun rise in the morning. Sometimes, the trails are closed off because of snow. Hikers can be hurt or even killed by snow and ice falling from the side of the mountain. People can plan their path using information on the mountain's website and warnings posted at the start of the trails.

ascend: to go up

avalanche: a dangerous event that happens when a lot of snow and ice fall down the side of a mountain

elevation: how high land is above the ocean

route: the path one takes

erupt: when a volcano explodes and lava and ash come out

snowcap: the top part of a mountain that is covered in snow

summit: the very top of a mountain

trailhead: the start of a trail

Writers sometimes use phrases with deep meanings in their writing. As you read more books and stories, you will become more and more familiar with these phrases. Here are a few useful phrases you can try using in your articles, essays, and stories.

Words From the Wise

Adages and **proverbs** are phrases that teach a lesson or give advice about life. Write the adage or proverb that goes with each scenario.

> birds of a feather flock together   (don't) put all your eggs in one basket

1. Jaime decided to try out for only one sports team. He's sure he will make the team.

_____

2. Brian and Ted have been friends since first grade. They both like comic books and superheroes.

_____

An **idiom** is a phrase that describes a situation in a funny way. Write the idiom that goes with each definition.

> piece of cake   fly off the handle

3. Calm down. There's no reason to _____ if you don't get your way.

4. Last night's homework was a _____. Jason finished it in no time.

Lesson 6: Revising and Editing

Objective
Students will make corrections and revisions to improve their writing, then produce a final copy.

Standards
With guidance and support from peers and adults, develop and strengthen writing as needed by planning, revising, editing, or rewriting.

What You Need
Copies of this packet for each student; whiteboard and markers

What to Do
1. Explain to students that before they can publish their writing, they need to revise and edit their work. During this phase, writers check their work and make any corrections. This step is important to make sure their writing has developed the topic, flows well, and is easy for readers to understand.

2. Display "Rules, Rules, Rules" (page 56) on the board and distribute copies to students. Have students correct the sentences on their paper. Then call on volunteers to come to the board and correct the mistakes on the sentences.

3. Distribute copies of the other activity pages in this section to give students additional practice in proofreading, revising, and editing. Then have them use the writing template (page 44) to write their final drafts.

Rules, Rules, Rules

Read the tips below. Fix and rewrite the sentences using the tips.

> **Punctuation**
> - Make sure every sentence has end punctuation.
> - Look for questions, and check that these sentences end with a question mark.

1. Campers can pour water on their campfire ashes to make sure the fire is put out

_____

2. How many state and national parks have you visited

_____

> **Spelling**
> - Look for words you know you usually misspell. Did you spell them correctly?
> - Use a dictionary or go online to check the spelling of words you do not know.

3. The bears in the forrest eat berrys and fishes.

_____

4. The hike threw the park is five milles long.

_____

> **Capitalization**
> - Capitalize all the proper nouns, like names of people and places.
> - Capitalize the nouns and verbs in your title.

5. ranger larry said to set up our tent in the section called tall oaks.

_____

6. "why we should love state parks"

_____

Use punctuation at the end of every sentence to show that the idea is finished.

Running in the Rain

Mandy wrote a paragraph about a girl who lives in the desert. She was so excited about her story that she forgot to write periods, exclamation points, and questions marks. Help her fix her paragraph by writing the correct punctuation in the boxes.

(1) Claire lives in the desert, where it does not rain very often ☐ (2) When Claire sees the sky get dark and hears thunder in the distance, she becomes very happy ☐ (3) Why ☐ (4) She knows it is going to rain soon ☐ (5) Her family arranges large barrels in their front yard to collect the rain water ☐ (6) Claire and her sister painted the rain buckets to make them very pretty ☐ (7) They use the water to wash the car and water their plants ☐ (8) This isn't why Claire is so happy, though ☐ (9) Why is she happy ☐ (10) She enjoys putting on her bathing suit and running around in the rain ☐

Adventures in the Park

Oh, no! All the punctuation disappeared from Diana's story. Help her get her draft ready by inserting the missing punctuation.

Where did all the ducks go Fiona didn't understand why there were no ducks in the lake

I don't know her brother said and I don't care

Fiona was used to her older brother's bad attitude Her mother was always reminding her that he was a teenager and teenagers are usually grumpy You know you can go play with your own friends right

Play My friends and I don't play Matt snorted

Maybe if you did you'd be happier Fiona decided she wanted to investigate why the ducks were missing She took a step closer to the edge of the water Where are they she wondered aloud

Maybe they're getting a hot dog

Fiona thought about what he said for a minute You're probably right Let's go look for them She stood up and started walking to the snack cart

There they are she said excitedly She had seen five white spots against the dark green grass. They walked closer to the cart and saw that two little girls were throwing pieces of bread to the ducks They were just hungry she said

I'm hungry too Let's get a snack while we're here

Anything to get you in a better mood Mr Grumpy

When you're unsure of what a word means or how to spell a word, a dictionary can come in handy. If there are a few words that you find very confusing, practice writing those words many times until you can spell them correctly without thinking.

Are These Words Confusing?

Circle the correct words in each sentence. Use a dictionary if you do not know the definitions.

1. I don't know *(weather/whether)* or not to believe the *(weather/whether)* report today.

2. *(I'll/Aisle)* sit in an *(I'll/aisle)* seat on the train.

3. *(There/They're)* are caterpillars in my flower garden. *(There/They're)* eating all of my leaves!

4. Only one shirt in the *(hole/whole)* box of old clothing had a *(hole/whole)* in it.

5. You can sit next *(to/two)* me because the bench is big enough for *(to/two)* people.

6. I sometimes *(write/right)* down information I read in books if I think it is *(write/right)* and interesting.

7. Ted *(threw/through)* his books in his bag when he was *(threw/through)* doing his homework.

8. In the *(passed/past)* year, I have learned how to play the clarinet well enough that I *(passed/past)* my skills test.

9. Did you hear George tell the very funny *(tail/tale)* about a boy with a very long *(tail/tale)*?

10. I *(except/expect)* everyone in the class to come to my party, *(except/expect)* Mary. She's going to be on vacation.

Name: _____   Date: _____

After you finish writing your draft, read your paragraph. Did you miss anything?

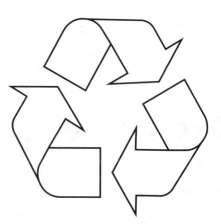

All About Recycling

Read Benjamin's draft and help him revise his writing. Use his notes to check that the facts are correct. Cross out the mistakes and write the correct information above them.

Our kitchen trash can is full of garbage, but some of that garbage can be recycled. My brother, who plays basketball, drinks a can of seltzer every afternoon after school. This afternoon, he threw away the soda can. He didn't recycle it, but he should have. By recycling one soda can, you can save a lot of electricity— enough to keep a microwave on for three hours! There are also a few plastic water bottles in the trash. Just one plastic bottle takes one thousand days to break down in a landfill. Let's recycle these! We get newspapers and magazines delivered every day. Did you know that we use about 69 tons of paper and paperboard in the United States each year? The good news is, about 67 percent of newspapers was recovered through recycling in 2013. We can do better! Make sure all your paper goes in the recycling bin. Better yet, use less paper!

FACT LIST

- Recycle a can of soda to power a television for three whole hours.

- In a landfill, plastic bottles require up to 1,000 years to completely break down.

- Every year, we use about 69 million tons of paper and paperboard in the United States.

The Woolworth Building

Belle is writing about New York City. Help her find mistakes, like words that are misspelled or not capitalized correctly. Use the editing marks below to correct the paragraph.

Add	∧	Take Out	ℓ	Small Letter	/
Period	⊙	Capital Letter	≡	Spelling Error	◯

One of my favorite skyscrapers in New York City is the Woolworth Building. It isn't the talest bulding in the city, so at one time it was. The Woolworth Building was designed by an artist named cass gilbert. Insid, the walls are decorated with gold and paintings. There is also Mosaics, which is a kind of art made using small, culored tiles instead of paint. The style of the building is called Gothic, and it looks sort of like a church. in fact, at 1916, a reverend officially named the building the "Cathedral of Commerce." This building is said to an symbol of American Business in the 20th century.

Answer Key

p. 8

Declarative: This weekend, the Westwood Kennel hosted a dog show for our community. It is a chance for dog owners to show off their animals and win prizes. Dogs of the same breed, or type, compete against one another. They are judged on their appearance. This dog show was held for a special purpose. It raised money for our local animal shelter. If you didn't attend the show, it's not too late to give.

Interrogative: Have you ever been to a dog show? Can you guess what it was?

Imperative: You should go to one sometime. Please donate to the shelter.

Exclamatory: It was a fun evening! The terrier group was the most fun to watch!

p. 9
Sample answers:

1. In the Black Hills region, which is located in South Dakota. → Mount Rushmore is in the Black Hills region, which is located in South Dakota.
2. About 400 workers and almost 15 years. → It took about 400 workers and almost 15 years to finish Mount Rushmore.
3. Wanted to show the presidents from the waist up, but there wasn't enough money. → He wanted to show the presidents from the waist up, but there wasn't enough money.
4. Two million visitors every year! → More than two million visitors come every year!

p. 10
1. A seed, which is small, can grow into a tree that is very tall.
2. My brother planted a sunflower, which grew very tall.
3. Sentences will vary.
4. Sentences will vary.

p. 11
2. It's always a good idea to map out your trip; there are apps that can help you.
2. You might want to go to an amusement park, or you could go to the beach.
3. Last year, Mom wanted to go to a national park, so we went to Yellowstone.
4. We got lost, since Dad got off the wrong exit.
5. Luckily we found a gas station, and the people there told us how to get back on the right road.

p. 12
Sample answers:

1. We planned to have a picnic on Saturday, but it started to rain.
3. We drove to the theater. There was a lot of traffic.
5. We gave up on that plan too. We went for pizza instead.

p. 13
Sample answers:

1. Even roots are dug out of the ground to spice our meals. → People even dig roots out of the ground to spice our meals.
2. Spices can be used in recipes whole and raw, like cloves of garlic, or they can be dried and made into a powder, such as turmeric powder. → You can use spices in recipes whole and raw, like cloves of garlic, or dry them and make them into a powder, such as turmeric powder.
3. Spices are used by cooks in their recipes to add special flavors. → Cooks use spices in their recipes to add special flavors.
4. Indian sauces are made using all kinds of spices. → Cooks use all kinds of spices to make Indian sauces.

p. 14
Sentence 2 uses correct punctuation.
1. "Put the cat down!" Kevin screamed. "He bites!"
3. Yesterday, my friend Gillian asked me, "Do you know what a monarch butterfly looks like?"
4. "The sun is way too bright," Lillian complained. "I need my sunglasses."
5. "Turn up the music," Jason said to his brother.
6. "Is anyone there?" Henry asked, not sure if he was alone in the dark room. "I sure hope this room isn't haunted."

p. 16
Sentences will vary.

p. 17
a. The ash gets in to the air, making it difficult to breathe.
d. People cannot easily escape an area when a volcano is erupting.
e. Hot lava can burn everything in its path, causing a lot of damage.

p. 18

Sentences will vary.

p. 19

For one thing; Despite this; In addition; Even though; But; As a result; In fact; On the contrary; However

p. 20

Paragraphs will vary.

p. 21

Concluding sentence: There are many ways we can reuse containers.
Sentences will vary.

p. 22

Sentences will vary.

p. 24

Answers will vary. Sample answers:
1. Denise should choose another topic that she finds more interesting.
2. Casey could keep digging for information, perhaps look for reports or complaints on the factory, or think of a different approach to the story.
3. Vincent should continue to write his topic, but he should make sure to include facts and details to support it.

p. 31

1. narrative   2. informative   3. opinion
4. narrative   5. informative

p. 32

1. sentence (1)
2. First, goats eat grass all day and all night. Second, goat poop would help our plants grow. Third, a goat could be trained to do work, like pulling a wagon.
3. a

p. 33

1. B   2. B   3. A   4. A   5. A   6. B   7. B   8. A

p. 34

Cross out 3 and 5.
Our food doesn't have to travel from faraway places.
Driving a car uses a lot of energy and releases tons of carbon dioxide into the atmosphere every year.
You waste energy when you keep the air conditioner on when you are not home.

p. 36

1. b   2. c   3. That's a terrible tragedy!
4. Answers will vary.
    Sample answer: What we can do to help

p. 38

1. setting   2. conflict   3. theme   4. plot
5. character

p. 39

Answers will vary.

p. 40

1. a   2. c   3. d   4. b

p. 41

1. First person; because the narrator used the pronouns *My, I,* and *me.*
2. I looked around my bedroom for my cell phone, but couldn't find it. If only I remembered that I had left it at my best friend's house.
3. Oh, no! Cary didn't jump high enough and didn't catch the ball. As she fell to the ground, the other team cheered, and her teammates put their heads down in shame.

p. 42

Sample answer:
One Saturday morning, Mom took Timmy and their dog Rufus to the park. When they got to the park, Rufus wouldn't stop barking.
Timmy asked Mom, "Why is Rufus barking?"
"I don't know," she replied. "Let's give Rufus some water and a treat." But the dog just kept barking.
"I don't think that worked," Timmy said. They had no idea what the dog wanted!
Rufus yipped one more time, and Mom finally understood! "Rufus wants to play fetch," Mom said. She laughed as she threw a stick. They played for a while, and then decided to go home for lunch.
"That was a lot of fun!" Timmy exclaimed.

p. 46

1. heavy   2. enormous   3. nervously   4. suddenly
5. frightened   6. glad   7. lucky   8. immediately
9. calm   10. exactly   11. proudly   12. beautiful

p. 47

1–5. Answers will vary.

p. 48

1. smell, sight, taste, hearing, touch
2–4. Sentences will vary.

p. 49

1. (are) destroyed, (would) happen
2. (is) covered, (are being) cut
3. (have) developed, (are) gone
4. (do) produce, (must) stop

p. 50

had been painting; was painting; was looking; will be erupting; was getting; am (just) finishing

p. 51

On the eastern coast; of Canada; with the Anne of Green Gables books; of the book; on the island; around the island; from the airport; across the water; to the island; from one side; of the island; to the other; within a short time; along the edge; of the island; Below the cliffs; at the edge; of the cliff; on top; of the world

p. 52

1. including   2. except that   3. because
4. due to   5. and besides   6. another

p. 53

Mt. Fuji is the tallest mountain in Japan. It is located outside Tokyo, Japan's capital city, and has an elevation of 12,388 feet. The mountain, which is usually pictured with a snowcap, is actually a volcano. The last time Mt. Fuji erupted was in 1707, a very long time ago.

A lot of people visit Mt. Fuji to hike. Visitors ascend to the summit to see the sun rise in the morning. Sometimes, the trails are closed off because of snow. Hikers can be hurt or even killed by an avalanche. People can plan their route using information on the mountain's website and warnings posted at the trailheads.

p. 54

1. put all your eggs in one basket
2. birds of a feather flock together
3. fly off the handle   4. piece of cake

p. 56

1. Campers can pour water on their campfire ashes to make sure the fire is put out.
2. How many state and national parks have you visited?
3. The bears in the forest eat berries and fish.
4. The hike through the park is five miles long.
5. Ranger Larry said to set up our tent in the section called Tall Oaks.
6. "Why We Should Love State Parks"

p. 57

1. .   2. ! or .   3. ?   4. .   5. .
6. .   7. .   8. .   9. ?   10. !

p. 58

Where did all the ducks go? Fiona didn't understand why there were no ducks in the lake.
"I don't know," her brother said, "and I don't care!"
Fiona was used to her older brother's bad attitude. Her mother was always reminding her that he was a teenager, and teenagers are usually grumpy. "You know you can go play with your own friends, right?"
"Play! My friends and I don't play!" Matt snorted.
"Maybe if you did, you'd be happier!" Fiona decided she wanted to investigate why the ducks were missing. She took a step closer to the edge of the water. "Where are they?" she wondered aloud.
"Maybe they're getting a hot dog."
Fiona thought about what he said for a minute.
"You're probably right. Let's go look for them." She stood up and started walking to the snack cart.
"There they are!" she said excitedly. She had seen five white spots against the dark green grass. They walked closer to the cart and saw that two little girls were throwing pieces of bread to the ducks. "They were just hungry," she said.
"I'm hungry too. Let's get a snack while were' here."
"Anything to get you in a better mood, Mr. Grumpy."

p. 59

1. whether, weather   2. I'll, aisle   3. There, They're
4. whole, hole   5. to, two   6. write, right
7. threw, through   8. past, passed   9. tale, tail
10. expect, except

p. 60

microwave → television; 1,000 days → 1,000 years; 69 tons → 69 million tons

p. 61

One of my favorite skyscrapers in New York City is the Woolworth Building. It isn't the tallest building in the city, but at one time it was. The Woolworth Building was designed by an artist named Cass Gilbert. Inside, the walls are decorated with gold and paintings. There are also mosaics, which are a kind of art made using small, colored tiles instead of paint. The style of the building is called Gothic, and it looks sort of like a church. In fact, in 1916, a reverend officially named the building the "Cathedral of Commerce." This building is said to be a symbol of American business in the 20th century.